Game Changers
Intrapreneurial Communication Strategies for Innovation

Table of Contents

Chapter 1. Introduction

Welcome to this exciting Special Report—the Game Changers: Intrapreneurial Communication Strategies for Innovation. Hold onto your hats for an exhilarating journey as we delve into the dynamic world of intrapreneurship! This report is primed to empower you with the practical skills to amplify innovation within your organization through the power of refined communication techniques. Dismiss the myth that entrepreneurship is an outside game only; you can be the catalyst of change right where you are. Encased within this extraordinary dossier are tested strategies, real-life case studies, and practical insights to unlock latent intrapreneurial spirit. Get ready to reshape your destiny, ignite your work environment, and drive unprecedented results. You'll be so thrilled by the insights in just the first few pages that you won't want to put it down! There's no time like the present to start revolutionizing your communication and craft your own stirring narrative of success. Stand by, because you're just one click away from making an exceptionally wise investment in your professional growth!

Chapter 2. Intrapreneurship: Understanding the Concept

The origins of intrapreneurship are closely linked with the business landscape of the late 20th century. The term 'intrapreneurship' was first coined by Gifford Pinchot III in 1978 and has ever since been associated with innovative activities within established organizations.

However, to fully grasp the importance and essence of intrapreneurship, first, we must grapple with the concept of entrepreneurship. It is fundamentally about venturing into the unknown, identifying opportunities, and accepting the risk in anticipation of enhanced reward. Entrepreneurs are typically hailed as pioneers of innovation in business models, products, services, and technologies. They are known to challenge traditional modes of operation, push boundaries, and endeavor relentlessly to create value.

2.1. What is Intrapreneurship?

Intrapreneurship is the practice of applying entrepreneurial skills and approaches within an existing organization. It leverages the constancy, resources, and market position of the organization to rapidly bring innovative ideas to fruition. Being an intrapreneur means you're a game changer in your company, possessing an entrepreneur's heart but operating within the established lines of a current company.

In an increasingly competitive environment, where disruptive technologies and business models challenge established conventions, intrapreneurship can be a critical differentiator, infusing the organization with agility, innovation, and resilience.

2.2. The Role of the Intrapreneur

Intrapreneurs are akin to organizational insurgents. They incubate transformative ideas and have the audacity to venture off established paths while still operating within an organizational framework. They often exhibit a strong sense of personal commitment to their ideas, galvanizing support, and aligning resources towards a shared vision.

Unlike entrepreneurs, intrapreneurs operate from a position of relative safety, shielded, to an extent, from potential downfalls. The initiative risk is largely borne by the organization; intrapreneurs can deviate from the norm and test new ideas and strategies without the fear of personal financial loss.

2.3. The Intrapreneurial Mindset

Intrapreneurship demands a distinct mindset. At its core is the ideal of corporate entrepreneurship, spurring entrepreneurial activity in a corporate setup, instilling a culture of exploration and innovation across the enterprise.

The intrapreneurial mindset is characterized by qualities such as initiative, resilience, and risk tolerance. It embraces curiosity and tenacity, necessitating an ability to question, challenge, and transform the status quo. Proactivity, combined with an insatiable desire to learn and adapt, differentiates the intrapreneurial mindset from others.

2.4. Intrapreneurship and Organizational Innovation

In the context of organizational innovation, intrapreneurship acts as a driving force. Intrapreneurs generate new business ideas and push for their implementation, often leading to new revenue streams and increased competitiveness. These efforts frequently translate into developing new products or services, improving processes, or penetrating new markets.

Innovations within organizations often result from intrapreneurial initiatives. By challenging traditional thinking and rules, intrapreneurs catalyze changes that lead to organizational growth and survival in the competitive marketplace.

2.5. Key Elements of Intrapreneurship

Intrapreneurship has three key elements—innovation, risk-taking, and proactiveness. It requires an innovative approach, as simply improving existing operations isn't enough. Innovation implies coming up with novel, creative ideas that can add significant value.

The second element is risk-taking. Just as entrepreneurs take risks, intrapreneurs must also be willing to accept a certain level of risk. They must have the courage to try new things even if there's a chance they might fail.

The third element is proactiveness. Intrapreneurs must be proactive, taking the initiative to identify opportunities and to act on them.

2.6. Encouraging Intrapreneurship

Encouraging intrapreneurship necessitates that organizations foster creative thinking, provide opportunities for initiative taking, and inject a tolerance for failure.

Cultures that permit employees to experiment without fearing failure or reprisal are fertile grounds for intrapreneurship. In this kind of environment, employees are more inclined to challenge traditional approaches, initiate changes, and bring innovative ideas on the table.

These trends encourage an intrapreneurial spirit that, while not without its challenges, holds immense potential in catalyzing innovation and driving organizational growth.

Intrapreneurship, thus, is an empowering process of fostering innovation, providing a platform upon which organizations can build to drive performance and competitiveness.

In conclusion, intrapreneurship is an invaluable tool for fostering innovation within organizations. It involves leveraging entrepreneurial approaches within the context of an existing organization. With the right mindset, risk-taking propensity, and proactive behavior, intrapreneurship can lead to significant improvement in organizational performance and competitiveness in the marketplace.

Chapter 3. Decoding Intrapreneurial Communication

"Strap in, as we launch into the nucleus of intrapreneurial success—communication. The articulation of ideas, strategies, and visions constitutes the backbone of innovation inside an organization. This extensive exploration will equip you with the framework to decode this pivotal aspect and utilize it to stimulate creativity and foster progression in your professional milieu. We'll dissect the concept, investigate its principles, and lay out a robust plan for superior intrapreneurial communication. So grab your notepads and get ready for an exciting ride.

3.1. The Essence of Intrapreneurial Communication

Communication isn't just about transmitting information—it's about creating understanding. In an intrapreneurial context, it's the touchstone for fostering a shared vision, ensuring transparency, and fostering an environment conducive to change. It's the lifeblood of innovation, driving idea exchange and collaboration essential for intrapreneurial activities.

In this space, the goal is to empower employees, facilitate knowledge sharing, and magnify the culture of innovation inside an organization. By cultivating open dialogue and lifting tacit boundaries, it bolsters adaptability and innovation readiness, enhancing the capability to transform ideas into tangible value.

Furthermore, intrapreneurial communication holds the key to stakeholder engagement and understanding of change. It facilitates the establishment of purpose, instills trust, and grooms intrapreneurial leaders, ensuring a smooth transition to an intrapreneurial culture.

3.2. The Central Pillars of Intrapreneurial Communication

Three core pillars define the robustness of intrapreneurial communication—clarity, empathy, and adaptability. Let's delve into these principles further.

1. Clarity is ensuring the sender's message is understood by the receiver as intended. For intrapreneurs, this isn't limited to conveying ideas but extended to conveying their value and potential. It's essential to be concise yet comprehensive, leaving no room for ambiguity.

2. Empathy, when infused into communication, breeds understanding and trust. It's understanding others' perspectives, experiences, and emotions to generate mutually beneficial outcomes. In intrapreneurial communication, empathy fosters an innovation-centric culture and nurtures collaborative networks.

3. Adaptability is the trait of adjusting communication based on the recipient's perspective and the situation's context. It is the ability to diversify messaging, tone, and delivery methods to achieve desired responses, crucial in intrapreneurial communication for navigating through varied stakeholders and situations.

3.3. A Practicable Guide for Mastering Intrapreneurial Communication

Now comes the crux of our journey— transforming this

understanding into practice. This section is an extensive guide to enhance your intrapreneurial communication prowess, structured in an easy-to-follow, step-wise format.

1. **Identify Key Stakeholders**: Understand who they are and what they seek from the innovation you propose. This is the first step towards tailored communication.

2. **Understand Communication Styles**: Stir versatility in your communication mix, adapting to the varied styles and preferences of your stakeholders.

3. **Craft Compelling Narratives**: People resonate with stories. Develop compelling narratives to showcase your ideas and their potential impact.

4. **Emphasize Transparency**: Create openness around your ideas, plans, and processes to build trust and facilitate shared decision making.

5. **Foster a Collaborative Network**: The roots of innovation lie in collaboration. Develop a network for idea exchange and collective evolution.

6. **Reiterate and Reciprocate**: Do not just transmit; engage in an active exchange of ideas, understand perspectives, and foster mutual growth.

3.4. Successful Strategies in Practice—Real-world Case Studies

Throughout the evolution of business, successful organizations have effectively leveraged intrapreneurial communication. Let's deduce lessons from these real-world case studies.

1. **Google and the Genesis of Gmail**: Google's open and collaborative communication strategy led to the development of innovative products like Gmail, conceived by an intrapreneur in

the company's "20% Time" initiative.

2. **IBM ThinkPlace**: IBM utilized a virtual suggestion box, promoting an open sharing culture. The result—an influx of innovative ideas enriching the organization's innovative pipeline.

3. **3M's Post-It Notes**: Art Fry's intrapreneurial initiative gave life to Post-It Notes. 3M's culture of open communication allowed this idea to be heard, developed, and ultimately commercialized.

The world waits for no one. Gear up and amplify your intrapreneurial communication prowess today! Remember, being an innovator doesn't mean you have to start outside; the true innovators are those who breathe life into ideas within their workspace."

Chapter 4. The Power of Intrapreneurial Communication

Innovation is the lifeblood of any thriving organization. It is this innovative spirit that births ground-breaking products, out-of-the-box business strategies, and marvels such as the Apple iPhone or Tesla's autopilot feature. But where does such innovation come from? Enter intrapreneurship—a concept where employees within organizations act as entrepreneurs, developing innovative ideas, products, and procedures that bolster the organization's growth. Central to this intrapreneurial process is communication. Effective intrapreneurial communication has the power to bake innovation into an organization's DNA, channelize productive brainstorming, influence decision-making processes, and shape your organization's future success.

4.1. Intrapreneurial Communication: The Bedrock of Innovative Environments

Intrapreneurial communication is much more than exchanging information; it is about forging connections, sharing vision, and fostering a creative and collaborative environment. It acts as the conduit that enables the diffusion of innovative ideas and strategies throughout an organization.

Communication underpins all stages of the innovation pipeline—from idea generation to implementation. An idea may be the genesis of an innovation, but without proper communication, it may amount to nothing. Shared understanding is the key here.

Imagine, you have a transformative idea to revolutionize a process within your organization. If you communicate it effectively, you will be able to better explain your vision, get feedback, build a team, raise resources, and influence decision-making, all of which are vital for successful innovation implementation.

Effective intrapreneurial communication also promotes a culture of innovation within the organization. It facilitates collaboration, encourages employees to share and discuss ideas and fosters an environment where every idea is valued. In this culture, innovation is not an isolated event but a continuous process.

4.2. Unleashing the Power of Effective Intrapreneurial Communication

To unleash the power of effective intrapreneurial communication, you need to understand its elements and nuances. Here are some pointers that may help you:

1. Clarity and Transparency: Clear and transparent communication nurtures trust and lays the foundation for collaboration and innovation. Make sure your ideas and objectives are articulated clearly, and all relevant information is shared transparently.

2. Active Listening: Active listening is an important part of intrapreneurial communication. When you listen to other's ideas and perspectives, it not only helps in improving your own ideas but also sends a signal across the organization that every idea and individual matters.

3. Empathy: Empathy can give wings to intrapreneurial communication. When you empathize with others and understand their perspectives, it helps in building strong relationships—the backbone of a collaborative and innovative

environment.

4. Adaptability: As an intrapreneur, it is crucial for you to adapt your communication style and strategies depending on the context, audience, and feedback.

4.3. Facilitating a Culture Shift: From Information Sharing to Intrapreneurial Communication

In many organizations, communication is mostly about information sharing. This is a culture that stifles innovation and creativity. Encouraging intrapreneurial communication requires a substantial shift in your organizational culture and communication practices.

1. Nurture an Open Environment: Encourage employees to voice their ideas, and assure them that their ideas will be taken seriously.

2. Encourage Collaboration: Encourage cross-departmental and cross-hierarchical collaborations. This enriches the diversity of ideas and promotes a holistic problem-solving approach.

3. Provide the Needed Support: Assure employees of your support, and make sure the needed resources—including time and budget—are available for the innovative ideas to take flight.

4.4. Intrapreneurial Communication in Action: Real-Life Case Studies

Several organizations have successfully harnessed the power of intrapreneurial communication for driving innovation. Google and 3M are two such examples.

Google encourages its engineers to spend 20% of their time on projects of their choosing, a practice that has birthed innovations like Gmail and Google Adsense. This is underpinned by open lines of communication where all Googlers can question, connect, and contribute.

3M's intrapreneurship program, dubbed Post-it Notes, was borne out of an engineer's need for a low-tack adhesive. This idea, initially rejected, was championed by a fellow employee who saw its potential. Guided by supportive and effective communication, this product became a market force and turned into a poster child for successful intrapreneurship.

4.5. Conclusion

Intrapreneurial communication is the secret sauce that can spur innovation and growth at unprecedented scales within organizations. But it requires the right understanding, continual efforts, and a conducive organizational culture. Start today, and open up a world of endless possibilities and growth for your organization. Because, when an idea meets the right communication, magic happens!

Remember, as an intrapreneur, your non-traditional ideas are the jewels that can add extraordinary value to your organization. It is up to you to share, shape, and bring those ideas into reality. And the most effective tool in your arsenal to do all this is powerful communication. So, articulate smartly, listen actively, empathize, collaborate, and watch the magic unfold!

Chapter 5. Leading Innovation: Commanding Intrapreneurial Efforts

In a corporate environment, innovation mostly champions from the leadership. To be sure, managers, executives and team leaders are empowered with the pivotal role of defining the direction, setting the pace, and encouraging every individual to contribute to the innovative narrative. Clearly, the command in driving intrapreneurial efforts is vested in the leadership. But how can they lead this charge effectively? What does it take to mobilize a team towards producing groundbreaking concepts that can revolutionize an entire organization? This section offers answers, strategies, and tools to tackle such questions.

5.1. Embracing and Cultivating a Culture of Innovation

A vital pillar to leading innovation is to encourage a culture of idea generation and entrepreneurship. To spark innovation, leaders must advocate for a safe culture that supports creativity, risk-taking, and inclusivity. This emphasis means relinquishing the fear of failure and imbuing a collective mindset that mistakes are stepping stones to learning and growth.

One way to cultivate a culture of innovation is by incorporating an intrapreneurial vision into the organization's mission statement. Additionally, adopting an open-door policy where employees can freely share their ideas and participate in decision-making processes is a tremendous morale booster. Employees who feel heard are more likely to contribute meaningful ideas that will drive innovation and, consequently, business growth.

5.2. Fostering Intrapreneural Skills within the Team

It's an accepted notion that anyone can harness intrapreneurial skills, provided they are given the right motivation and resources. As a leader, you are in a prime position to foster these skills within your team members.

One possible approach is through capacity-building activities, such as innovation workshops or hackathons, where employees can brainstorm ideas, learn from each other, and figure out how to transform those ideas into action. Another way is by setting up mentorship programs where seasoned intrapreneurs within the organization can guide newer members, thus cultivating a learn-and-grow atmosphere.

Encouraging employees to collaborate cross-functionally can also yield excellent results. Such collaborations often lead to new ideas that might not have emerged if teams remained within their silos. As various perspectives converge, creativity slingshots, and the propensity for innovation amplifies.

5.3. Implementing Intrapreneurial Ideas - Navigating Through the Complexities

Execution forms a crucial part of the innovation process. A great concept can only be appreciated when it's turned into a product, service, or an operational change. However, the step of implementing intrapreneurial ideas often comes with its complexities.

Leaders must understand that not every idea will become a reality due to operational, financial, or resource constraints. The trick lies in identifying the most viable ideas that align with the company's strategic goals and have the potential to add tangible value. Rigorous evaluation mechanisms, such as using an idea metrics chart that measures an idea's feasibility, novelty, and relevance can be instrumental in this process.

Additionally, having a proper framework for implementation that includes phases of development, quality testing, pilot testing, and clear timelines will set the path for successful execution. Flexibility should be infused in this framework, given the dynamic nature of innovation where adjustments, iterations, or pivots may be needed along the way.

5.4. The Intrapreneurial Leader - Being the Role Model

Lastly, leadership plays a major role in setting an example. The intrapreneurial leader is both a navigator and an enabler. On one hand, they guide the process of innovation, keep the goals aligned, and engage the organization's resources optimally. On the other hand, they foster an environment where creativity and intrapreneurship can flourish.

The dynamic leader does more than instruct; they inspire and motivate their teams. Leaders should live the spirit of innovation they wish to induce. When leaders demonstrate their commitment to an intrapreneurial culture by endorsing new ideas, persisting despite failure, and celebrating successes—no matter how small—they amplify the message that innovation is not only accepted but welcomed and rewarded.

Embodying intrapreneurial qualities and showcasing them through action—risk-taking, thinking beyond set frameworks or encouraging out-of-the-box solutions—emphasizes the message and image of a leader who is in the spearhead of the company's innovative struggles and triumphs.

Intrapreneurship isn't an overnight journey; it's an ongoing process that requires continuous support, nurturing, and resilience. Through effective communication, solid culture, capacitation activities, prudent evaluation and implementation, and, most importantly, leading by example, you're well on your way to commanding your team's intrapreneurial efforts.

Chapter 6. Case Studies: Intrapreneurial Communication in Action

An in-depth exploration of intrapreneurial communication necessitates a close examination of real-life instances that illustrate its power in bringing about innovation. This section presents exemplary case studies from various industries where intrapreneurial communication has not only amplified innovation but also fostered an environment that encourages continuous learning and growth.

6.1. Communication Strategies at Google

Google has consistently ranked as one of the top companies worldwide for innovation. This isn't by accident: there's a fervent intrapreneurial spirit embedded within Google's DNA, largely attributable to its distinct communication strategies. A key feature of their strategy is the emphasis on openness and transparency. The widely recognized 'TGIF' meetings where all employees, irrespective of their titles and roles, are updated about company affairs and future plans, contribute to their invigorating intrapreneurial environment. They've managed to build a culture where everyone feels a part of the larger mission, enabling them to think creatively and take calculated risks for innovation.

6.2. Encouraging Dialogue at Pixar

Pixar Animation Studios has been creating magical experiences for decades. At the heart of this creative force is their unique intrapreneurial communication practice. They've established 'The Braintrust', a candid session where the directors and key personnel discuss the progress of ongoing projects. These meetings are not for authority figures to pass judgment, rather they're designed for everyone to openly express their viewpoints, fostering an environment of candid feedback and collective brainstorming. By not focusing on hierarchy, Pixar has created a culture where every voice counts, driving extraordinary innovation and unparalleled success in animation.

6.3. Flat Hierarchies at Valve

Video game development company Valve Corporation flaunts a flat organizational structure where job titles barely matter. This structure aids in promoting open and direct communication between members, bypassing perceived barriers typically created by hierarchies. Employees are not only motivated to express their ideas, but they're also empowered to pursue projects they're passionate about. This kind of intrapreneurial communication has led Valve to produce groundbreaking video games that have disrupted the market and set new standards in the gaming world.

6.4. Cross-Functional Communication at Spotify

Spotify's innovative approach to internal communication is underpinned by its formation of dynamic 'squads', 'tribes', and 'guilds'. This structure enables cross-functional communication and collaboration, allowing individuals with diverse skill sets to come together and contribute to shared goals. This has led to a culture of intrapreneurship at Spotify, with teams autonomously tuning into customer insights and responding with groundbreaking features like Discover Weekly and Spotify Wrapped.

6.5. Enabling Freedom of Speech at Toyota

Toyota's intrapreneurial communication style manifests through the 'Toyota Way' — a set of principles that puts respect for people at its core. They implement Hansei (self-reflection) and Kaizen (continuous improvement), encouraging employees at all levels to speak up and suggest improvements. This kind of inclusive communication has been instrumental in Toyota's ability to continuously innovate and maintain its position as a market leader in the automobile industry.

6.6. Promotion of Idea Sharing at 3M

At 3M, a company known for its wealth of innovative products, the '15% Rule' allows employees to spend a certain amount of their work time on projects of their choice. This policy has fostered an environment of experimentation, leading to groundbreaking inventions like Post-it Notes. 3M's intrapreneurial communication strategy creates a space where individuals can freely share and explore ideas, often leading to exciting new products.

All these case studies are a testament to the transformative effect of intrapreneurial communication in fostering innovation within an organization. The common thread among these success stories is the cultivation of an open, fluid, and empowering communication environment that galvanizes individuals to turn creative ideas into reality. It's not just about allowing creativity, rather it's about harmoniously linking cross-functional teams, bridging gaps, discarding hierarchies, encouraging dialogue, and letting the thrill of exploration and the reward of innovation be everyone's business. These strategies can be applied across any industry and scaled to fit any business size to promote intrapreneurial culture and consequently, innovation. The challenge is not in understanding these methods, but in their implementation, in the integration of these practices into the very fabric of an organization's culture. It's time to start empowering communication in your organizations and embark on an unprecedented journey of intrapreneurship and innovation.

Chapter 7. Pillars of Effective Intrapreneurial Communication

Throughout this comprehensive exploration, we'll unpack the foundational elements behind inventive communication that allows for transformative intrapreneurial growth and progress. The pillars touched upon will span from the beautifully nuanced interplay between listening and engaging, to embracing ambiguity, harnessing the power of storytelling, orchestrating synergistic collaboration, and leveraging emotional intelligence for effective communication.

7.1. The Prime Minister: Listening and Engaging

The first two keystones of effective intrapreneurial communication are listening and engaging. Effective listening forms the basis upon which the following conversational engagement is built. An intrapreneur needs to listen actively, genuinely digesting different perspectives and insights shared by their co-workers. This fundamental understanding will form the foundation for constructing responses, asking questions, and engaging in productive dialogue.

Engagement, on the other hand, is catalytic. Authentic engagement involves participating actively in the conversation, showing your commitment by contributing thoughtfully and demonstrating respect for all participants' ideas. The two-way nature of communication becomes central here, with the interplay between listening and engaging facilitating a dynamic, collaborative exchange of views and ideas where creativity can thrive.

7.1.1. Listening as an Active Art

Active listening is not a passive occupation; it's an art. It is about making the speaker feel understood and valued, ensuring their words are deciphered correctly, and their ideas are meaningfully interpreted. Listening is paying undivided attention to the words, tones, and nuances, aiming for comprehension rather than just awaiting your turn to speak.

7.1.2. Foster Genuine Engagement

Effective engagement requires consistent, deliberate actions. Every interaction should reflect a commitment to a common goal, whether it's brainstorming ideas, working on a task, or resolving a challenge. Engagement puts everyone on an equal footing, dissolving hierarchical barriers and empowering all team members.

7.2. Storytelling: A Powerful Communicative Armour

Stories have the power to communicate complex ideas in a compelling, relatable way—a characteristic that makes them an essential tool in the intrapreneurial communication arsenal. An adept intrapreneur uses storytelling to communicate their ideas, share their vision, or pitch their innovative projects and strategies.

Storytelling is an important part in creating riveting narratives around the ideas, stirring emotions and galvanizing action. Stories have a way of engendering an emotional connect, engaging the listener in a strategic conversation and sparking innovative dialogue.

7.3. Embracing Ambiguity and Uncertainty

Innovation is inherently bound with ambiguity and unpredictability. Thus, effective intrapreneurial communicators must be comfortable with uncertainty, using it as a launch pad for creativity instead of a barrier for progress.

7.3.1. Navigating through Ambiguity

For an intrapreneur, the unknown is not a realm of fear; rather, they see it as a realm of possibilities. Navigate ambiguity by reframing it as an open-ended question that inspires innovative solutions.

7.3.2. Uncertainty as a Catalyst for Innovation

Uncertainty should be viewed as a space brimming with creative potential. An intrapreneur adapts to changes, leverages uncertain situations to their advantage, and shapes spontaneous ideas into structured, executable plans.

7.4. Collaboration: Sowing Seeds of Synergy

Innovation thrives when minds meet, mingle, and meld ideas to create something exceptional. Effective intrapreneurial communication thus deeply cherishes and fosters collaboration. By intentionally cultivating openness, a sense of community, and mutual respect, intrapreneurs encourage synergistic collaboration – the kind that leads to groundbreaking innovation.

7.5. Emotional Intelligence: The Unsung Hero

Emotional intelligence is indispensable to effective intrapreneurial communication. Being an emotionally intelligent communicator means recognizing, understanding, and managing your emotions and those around you. This sensitivity allows for more empathetic communication, diffusing tension, boosting morale, and fostering a more engaging, productive workspace.

Intrapreneurial communication strategies can greatly influence individual and organizational success. As we've discussed, these key pillars—active listening and engagement, storytelling, embracing ambiguity, fostering collaboration, and leveraging emotional intelligence—are pivotal in creating a conducive environment for intrapreneurial innovation.

These pillars are not independent, instead, they interweave and coincide to create a dynamic and fluid art of communication—an art that can steer the destiny of innovations. Now, take these pillars and construct your own edifice of successful intrapreneurial communication. Remember, the power to bring about change lies within you, and effective communication is your vehicle.

Chapter 8. Strategies for Fostering a Communication-based Intrapreneurial Culture

The foundation of an intrapreneurial culture largely relies on robust, thought-out, and effective communication strategies. By enhancing transparency and openness, firms not only empower their employees but also foster an environment where innovation takes precedence.

8.1. Building a Transparent and Open Culture

Unleashing the power of intrapreneurship in an organization requires fostering an open and transparent environment. This openness facilitates the free flow of knowledge, ideas, and feedback among different organizational levels. A culture of transparency is crucial because it fosters trust and encourages employees to be proactive, take calculated risks, and share their creative ideas.

Employers should start by establishing clear communication channels that disseminate essential information about corporate goals, values, and changes promptly. They should also encourage team members to ask questions, share insights, and feel comfortable addressing their concerns. In this encouraging atmosphere, employees are more likely to help drive organizational innovation.

8.2. Encouraging Agile Communication

The agile methodology that initially brought revolution in the software industry has valuable lessons for corporate communication too. Agile communication aims to optimize efficiency, productivity, and satisfaction among project teams in business environments.

Agile communication fosters a fundamentally decentralized and flexible communication structure that involves daily stand-ups, allowing for real-time problem-solving. This quick and iterative approach to communication aids in weeding out any latent issues and spurs innovative thinking. For intrapreneurial culture to thrive, agility and adaptability are non-negotiable.

8.3. Advocating for Two-Way Communication

Even the most well-formulated message can miss its mark if it is sent one-way. Two-way communication fosters idea exchanges and eliminates the conventional top-down approach in a professional environment. It transforms employees into active participants, enabling them to voice their opinions, suggest changes, and effectively contribute to discussions related to the shaping of the organization.

By implementing platforms like town-hall meetings, regular surveys, brainstorming sessions, and open forums, organizations can develop a two-way communication loop. This reciprocal flow eases the process of introduction and acceptance of new ideas.

8.4. Creating Safe Spaces for Idea Sharing

Inaugurating physical and virtual platforms where employees can share their innovative ideas is quintessential in promoting a culture of intrapreneurship. Spaces like these inspire employees to engage, share, and collaborate on new projects and ideas without fear of criticism or failure.

Such platforms also serve as a catalyst for fostering healthy relationships among employees from different departments, promoting cross-pollination of ideas. When employees from diverse backgrounds and experiences interact, they create a rich array of ideas. This diversity and inclusion in idea generation are the lifeblood of intrapreneurial culture.

8.5. Promoting Intrapreneurial Success Stories

Promoting and applauding intrapreneurial success stories is another way to foster this culture within the company. Its purpose is multi-fold. Firstly, it keeps the employees informed about ongoing innovations, helping them feel involved in the organization's successes. Secondly, it motivates them to replicate the behavior of intrapreneurs who have achieved success. Lastly, the narrative helps to embed the concept of intrapreneurship into the company's ethos, making it a part of the company culture organically.

8.6. Emphasizing the Importance of Feedback

In the context of a communication-based intrapreneurial culture, initiating timely feedback loops holds prime importance. This can be done through performance reviews, one-on-one interactions, and team debriefs. Constructive feedback not only paves the way for personal growth but also helps identify the areas that can be refined at the organizational level. Feedback helps a company take its intrapreneurship game from good to great, by being an incremental process that aids in constant evolution.

In conclusion, fostering a communication-based intrapreneurial culture requires a paradigm shift from traditional communication methods. It requires an inclination towards transparency and openness, agile communication, two-way communication, creating safe spaces, promoting intrapreneurial success, and emphasizing feedback. With these strategies in place, organizations have a solid mode of action to create an environment that is ripe for intrapreneurial success.

Chapter 9. Overcoming Challenges: Navigating Barriers to Intrapreneurial Communication

Despite the abundant opportunities for innovation within organizations, intrapreneurship is often riddled with numerous obstacles. These impediments might be inherent in an organization's structure, culture, or even originate from the individuals themselves. However, embracing change is quintessential for growth, and organizations that empower and encourage their employees to exercise intrapreneurship often jump the hurdle and rise to greatness.

9.1. Embrace Risk to Foster Innovation

Risk and innovation are two sides of the same coin. Without some degree of risk-taking, organizations can stifle their innovative prowess. While it's common for organizations to discourage failure, considering it as an opposite to success, savvy organizations acknowledge that failure is not an endpoint, but a springboard for innovation.

Understanding and embracing risk, in a calculated manner, can significantly reinforce your intrapreneurial communication strategies. Convey to your team that failures are simply stepping stones towards the organization's progress by uncompromisingly sharing information about both successful and failed ventures. Transparency not only lightens the fear of failure among individuals but also creates a resilient culture where teams feel safe to innovate.

9.2. Decentralize Decision Making

Typically, organizations centralize decision-making structures and restrict authority within a limited team. While this might seem like a convenient option, it hampers the sharing of ideas and inhibits intrapreneurship. Consider decentralizing decision making and promoting an open dialogue about new ideas within your organization.

Also, engage team members in crafting solutions to the company's challenges. The sense of ownership and confidence this instills can lead to significant results. Acknowledge and respect varied perspectives without isolating any voice, promoting an ecosystem of respect, mutual growth, and hence more effective intrapreneurial communication.

9.3. Establish an Intrapreneur-friendly Organizational Culture

Organizational culture has a profound influence on how the workforce communicates, innovates, and takes risks. A work environment that provides employees the freedom to express ideas, experiment, and prototype without the fear of criticism encourages intrapreneurial spirit.

On the contrary, a stifling culture that doesn't embrace change or is obsessed with maintaining the status quo can hinder intrapreneurship. As an intrapreneur, it is critical to understand the existing organizational culture and take comprehensive action to gradually transform it towards a more innovation-friendly environment.

9.4. Mastering Effective Communication

Intrapreneurial communication is the core that enables individuals and organizations to surface and implement innovative ideas effectively. It is a multi-faceted process that involves conveying the concepts, strategies, or projects to various stakeholders within the organization.

To facilitate effective communication, be sure to articulate your ideas clearly, persuasively, and in a way that aligns with the organization's broader goals. Additionally, consider the audience and its frame of reference when crafting your message. Tailoring your communication to meet the needs and expectations of your audience can help gain their buy-in and support.

9.5. Recognizing and Overcoming Obstacles

The intrapreneurial journey will feature a plethora of hurdles and bottlenecks. However, recognizing these challenges is the first crucial step towards overcoming them. Whether these obstacles are structural, such as rigid hierarchies and policies, or cultural hurdles like the fear of failure and risk-aversion, it is essential to confront them head-on and implement the necessary measures to circumvent them.

In conclusion, understanding, embracing, and navigating these barriers with a strong communication strategy at the helm can empower you and your team to innovate within your organization. Remember, the key to impactful intrapreneurship lies in effective communication, comprehensive risk management, an open work culture, and the tenacity to overcome challenges. With these guiding pillars, you're all set to script your organization's impressive journey towards growth and innovation.

Chapter 10. Emerging Trends: Future of Intrapreneurial Communication

The constant surge of innovation is a significant hallmark of the modern world, reflecting the importance of proactive change and progress. This relentless pursuit of innovation has given rise to a subculture within corporate ecosystems—Intrapreneurship. As we experience a shift in communication paradigms, it is of utmost importance to assess the emerging trends in intrapreneurial communication, which forms the essence of this elaborate discussion.

10.1. The Rise of Digital Communication Platforms

The last decade has been a testament to the transformative power of digital technology. In particular, the role of digital communication channels in fostering intrapreneurial spirit cannot be overstated. Digital platforms have demolished boundaries and timelines, making inter-departmental and inter-organizational communication much more streamlined, spontaneous, and persistent. Intranet, Instant Messaging, Emails, and Customized Workflow Applications are just a few examples of communication platforms that have revolutionized inter-departmental connect, boosting intrapreneurship.

10.2. The Importance of Social Networking for Intrapreneurs

The advent of corporate social networking has significantly aided in the metamorphosis of traditional corporate landscapes. Often, an intrapreneur's journey is born out of casual interactions or "water cooler conversations." Platforms like Yammer, Slack, and Microsoft teams have digitalized these exchanges, allowing for serendipitous interactions even with remote teams. Fostering collaboration and innovation, these platforms are shaping the future of intrapreneurial communication by opening pathways for unbounded exchange of ideas.

10.3. Embracing Multimodal Communication

The future of intrapreneurial communication foresees an increasing reliance on multimodal communication—where text, symbols, videos and icons co-occur, creating inclusive communicative spaces. This shift to mix modes of communication allows for the comprehensive representation of concepts and ideas, easing the understanding of complex innovation concepts, especially in a diverse and global workforce. Leveraging multimodal communication helps in building unity, stimulating creativity, and ensuring the creation of innovative solutions that resonate with diverse stakeholders.

10.4. Interplay of Technology and Emotional Intelligence

Intrapreneurship demands a fine balance between technological acumen and emotional intelligence. Cultivating empathy, understanding cultural nuances, active listening, and emotion recognition are crucial elements of intrapreneurial communication. These skills enable intrapreneurs to nurture an ecosystem that supports risk-taking, collaboration, inclusivity, and innovation. Advancements in AI and ML have ushered in a new era of tools capable of emotion analytics, sentiment analysis, and intuitive communication assistants, helping intrapreneurs navigate the emotional landscape of their workspaces successfully.

10.5. Transparency and Two-way Communication

In an increasingly connected world, transparency and open-door communication are becoming the norm. The future necessitates communication models that focus on dialogue instead of monologue. Encouraging two-way communication initiates peer discussions, encourages ideation, builds trust, and promotes intrapreneurial spirit. Building platforms for a healthy exchange of ideas not only stimulates creativity but also ensures that every voice is heard and valued.

In conclusion, the future of intrapreneurial communication will be defined by evolving communication trends powered by sophisticated digital technology and a greater understanding of emotional intelligence. The blend of these elements—coupled with a deep emphasis on dialogue, collaboration, and inclusive thinking—will lead to enriched intrapreneurial ecosystems within organizations, fostering a culture of persistent innovation and growth.

Chapter 11. Bringing It All Together: Implementing Intrapreneurial Communication Strategies

From the innovative brainstorming sessions to carefully planned strategy development, turning an intrapreneurial vision into a ground-breaking reality depends heavily on implementing effective communication strategies. Armed with these skills, you can confidently navigate through the organizational labyrinth, driving successful change and innovation.

11.1. The Prerequisite: Establishing A Culture of Communication

A culture that fosters open dialogue and encourages the free flow of ideas is the backbone of intrapreneurship. It fuels the thinking tanks, fosters trust, and encourages team members to voice their innovative ideas without fear of reprisal. As such, the first step in this journey is to lay a solid foundation of strong, open communication among all stakeholders.

To embed this culture:

1. Foster an environment of inclusiveness - Different perspectives can unearth fresh and diverse solutions. Therefore, inclusion should be the cornerstone upon which your corporate communications adopt a horizontal rather than a traditional vertical flow.

2. Encourage transparency - Transparency removes any hint of secrecy, fostering trust among team members.

3. Establish open-door policies - This encourages casual communication, offering a platform to freely share brilliant ideas that might otherwise remain dormant.

11.2. Putting The Spotlight on Active Listening

As an intrapreneur, simply hearing your employees is not enough; you need to listen actively. This implies paying attention not only to what's being said, but also how it's being said, while observing body language and nuances in communication.

To flex your active listening muscles:

1. Show empathy - Attempt to understand diverse perspectives.

2. Be patient - Give the speaker time to articulate their thoughts.

3. Provide feedback - Feedback demonstrates that you've comprehended the message.

11.3. Adopting The Art of Persuasive Communication

As an intrapreneur, you're not only a vision provider but also its chief motivator. The art of persuasion demonstrates your commitment to your vision, influences others to share your enthusiasm, and aligns them towards your goal.

To enhance persuasive communication:

1. Be passionate - Passion is infectious; it draws people in and persuades them to believe in your vision.

2. Use storytelling - Stories not only capture attention but also help others visualize the goal.

3. Use simple, compelling language - Clear, concise, and jargon-free communication helps everyone understand your message, regardless of their roles in the organization.

11.4. Embracing Technology in Communication

In today's digital landscape, technology must be leveraged in intrapreneurial communication strategies. Communication tools and platforms can foster collaboration, encourage idea sharing, and enable real-time updates.

Choosing the right technology:

1. Align with the team's needs - The choice of digital tools should factor in the needs of your team facilitating empathetic, user-friendly approaches to communication.
2. Be adaptable - Fast-paced technological changes demand adaptability.
3. Evaluate regularly - Regular checks help ensure the technology platforms are meeting your communication needs.

11.5. Effective Cross-Functional and Multilevel Communication

The ability to relay information accurately while addressing each element in the organizational matrix, such as cross-functional teams or different hierarchical levels, often determines the success of an intrapreneur's endeavor.

For effective cross-functional and multilevel communication:

1. Understand the unique needs of each group - Tailored messages

resonate better with diverse groups.

2. Leverage champions in each team - These champions can act as ambassadors for your vision within their respective teams, ensuring buy-in at all levels.

3. Harness the power of informal channels - This can help eliminate potential obstacles, including the idea-blocking hierarchy.

Implementing these strategies can sometimes feel like a daunting task. However, with consistent practice and commitment, the journey from envisioning a radical idea to witnessing its fruition can be a rewarding experience. By fostering the right communication culture, actively listening and persuading others, leveraging technology, and managing complex networks, you are setting stage for an intrapreneurial revolution in your organization. Observing the changes in your team—and in yourself—will be worth every step along this captivating journey.